Original title:
The Poetry of Cities

Copyright © 2024 Creative Arts Management OÜ
All rights reserved.

Author: Tim Wood
ISBN HARDBACK: 978-9916-88-080-7
ISBN PAPERBACK: 978-9916-88-081-4

Vibrant Corners

In bustling streets, colors collide,
Life dances brightly, nothing to hide.
Laughter echoes, joy fills the air,
Every corner whispers stories to share.

Children play under the sun's warm embrace,
Artists create, each line finds its place.
Flavors of spices waft in the breeze,
Vibrant corners invite hearts to tease.

City Lights and Long Nights

Neon glows paint the night sky,
Dreamers wander, letting time fly.
Every heartbeat, a pulse in the dark,
City lights shimmer, igniting a spark.

Sidewalks hum with tales untold,
Whispers of secrets, both young and old.
Stars above, a distant array,
Long nights linger, the world in a sway.

Stories Beneath the Surface

Beneath the waves, silence thrives,
Ancient tales where mystery dives.
Echoes of ships, lost in the blue,
Secrets of time, a world anew.

Coral gardens, vibrant and vast,
Life weaving memories of the past.
Gentle currents dance with grace,
Stories unfold in this hidden place.

Urban Reveries

In the city's heart, dreams quietly bloom,
Concrete jungles dispel all gloom.
Windows aglow with life and with light,
Urban reveries take flight at night.

Voices intertwine, a melodic sound,
In every moment, magic is found.
Yet still, in the shadows, dreams can ignite,
A tapestry woven, bold and bright.

Silhouettes at Dawn

Figures dance in morning light,
Shadows stretch with gentle might.
Whispers carried by the breeze,
Nature wakes with quiet ease.

Colors blend in soft embrace,
Each hue finds its rightful place.
Day awakens, night retreats,
Silhouettes in dawn's soft beats.

Whispers of the Skyline

Steel and glass reach for the sky,
Voices mingle, passing by.
City dreams in twilight glow,
A tapestry of ebb and flow.

Echoes of the day unfold,
Stories waiting to be told.
In the shadows, secrets lie,
Beneath the vast and open sky.

Rhythm of the Streets

Footsteps tap in syncopate,
Life's pulse beats, can't hesitate.
Banners wave in vibrant hues,
Every moment tells the news.

Laughter rings from every lane,
Joy and sorrow intertwined remain.
In the heartbeat of the crowd,
Voices rise, both soft and loud.

Lanterns in the Mist

Flickering lights in morning haze,
Guiding paths through quiet ways.
Each lantern holds a tale untold,
Illuminating hearts so bold.

In the fog, they softly gleam,
Casting glow like a shared dream.
Whispers float on chilly air,
Guiding souls who wander there.

The Breath of the Boulevard

Beneath the whispering trees, night grows,
Where lanterns flicker soft like dreams.
The pavement hums a tune of old,
Stories shared by lovers' gleams.

Stars dangle low with secrets kept,
In shadows cast by time's embrace.
Footsteps echo, hearts are swept,
In the dance of this sacred space.

Cool breezes stir with laughter's light,
As strangers pass with knowing smiles.
Each corner holds a spark of night,
A moment's pause that lingers miles.

In twilight's glow, the world feels right,
As dreams take flight on whispered sighs.
The boulevard breathes pure delight,
A canvas painted by our eyes.

Rain on Pavement Echoes

Drops dance lightly on the street,
Whispers of memories rise and meet.
Each splash sings a silent song,
A rhythm that carries us along.

Clouds drift softly, shadows play,
Painting the world in shades of gray.
Footsteps wander, lost in thought,
While nature's art is quietly sought.

Reflections shimmer in puddles deep,
Stories of those who once did weep.
Echoes linger, a fleeting sound,
As hearts awaken from lost ground.

The scent of earth, fresh and new,
Meets the city, as if to renew.
In the rain, we find what we crave,
A moment of peace, a gentle wave.

The Pulse of Public Square

Voices rise, a chorus loud,
People gather, a vibrant crowd.
Laughter mingles with the air,
In the heart of the square, we share.

A street performer strums a tune,
Under the watch of the golden moon.
Children dance, joy intertwined,
In the pulse of life, all aligned.

News and tales are passed along,
In every face, a story strong.
Dreams collide, and hope ignites,
In this space of shared delights.

As day turns into night's embrace,
The public square holds every face.
A tapestry of lives unfurled,
The pulse of a united world.

Hidden Gardens in Grey

Amidst the concrete and steel walls,
Whispers of green break urban calls.
A secret space where silence dwells,
In hidden corners, nature swells.

Petals peek through a cracked stone,
Life's tenacity, clearly shown.
In shadows cast by towering trees,
A refuge found in the gentle breeze.

Moss blankets paths, soft and serene,
In the stillness, a tranquil scene.
Each blossom tells a tale unsung,
In quiet gardens, life is sprung.

A lone bench invites a weary soul,
To breathe, to ponder, to feel whole.
In hidden gardens, peace is found,
A gentle heartbeat, nature's sound.

Wall Murals and Dreams

Colors burst on weathered walls,
Tales of life where silence calls.
Each stroke of paint, a story told,
In murals bright, our dreams unfold.

Voices echo through the lanes,
Art reflects our joys and pains.
A canvas vast across the stone,
In every hue, we find our own.

Children laughing, dancers free,
Life's vibrance captured, endlessly.
In shades of hope, despair, and love,
A glimpse of heaven shining above.

The street becomes a gallery sought,
Where every mural connects each thought.
In wall murals, a shared embrace,
A dreamer's heart finds its place.

Remnants of Rain

Droplets dance on cobblestones,
Whispers of a fleeting storm.
Shadows stretch as daylight wanes,
Nature's fresh and tranquil form.

Puddles mirror clouds above,
Reflecting dreams that slip away.
In their depths, the world of love,
Echoes of the skies at play.

Petals glisten, earth's embrace,
A symphony of soft refrains.
In each corner, traces trace,
The longing sigh of lingering rains.

Lights in the Gloom

Flickers dance in the darkest night,
Stars emerge to spark delight.
In the alleys, shadows creep,
Hope ignites from dreams we keep.

Each small flame, a story told,
Fading whispers, brave and bold.
In the quiet, courage grows,
Guiding hearts where no one knows.

Through the fog, a path appears,
With each step, we face our fears.
In the gloom, we find our way,
Lights that lead through night to day.

Unfolding Landscapes

Mountains rise, a silent hymn,
Valleys breathe, horizons brim.
Fields of gold, waves of green,
Nature's brush, a tranquil scene.

Rivers carve through ancient stone,
Stories etch the land's own throne.
Skies shift hues, embrace the dawn,
Colors weave where dreams are drawn.

Whispers of the wind go far,
In each corner, peace a scar.
Unfolding tales in earth and sky,
Landscapes breathe, and so do I.

Voices of the Unseen

Echoes rise from vanished days,
Silhouettes in softest haze.
Silent songs that never cease,
Threads of life in quiet peace.

Whispers weave through branches bare,
Tales of heart woven with care.
In the stillness, spirits roam,
Yearning for a distant home.

Voices call from places lost,
Memories that weave and frost.
In the shadows, truth remains,
Bridges built through love's refrains.

Neon Heartbeats

In the city where dreams ignite,
Neon glows in the deep of night.
Rhythms pulse in electric air,
Whispers of hope linger everywhere.

Each heartbeat syncs with the light,
Drawing lovers into the flight.
Colors dance on the wet street tiles,
Alive with laughter, alive with smiles.

Moments captured in flashing frames,
Every soul plays their vibrant games.
Under stars that shimmer and spark,
We find our way out of the dark.

Shadows of the Past

In quiet corners of the mind,
Memories left behind unwind.
Echoes whisper through the trees,
Carrying tales upon the breeze.

Figures wane in twilight's glow,
Fading phantoms, haunting slow.
Time's embrace is gentle, yet tight,
Holding secrets, lost from sight.

A picture frames the days gone by,
Captured moments that make us sigh.
In the silence, lessons dwell,
Shadows tell the stories well.

Dancers in the Alley

Beneath the moon, they sway and spin,
With every step, both lost and win.
Graffiti walls their canvas bold,
Where dreams are painted, bright and gold.

The rhythm pulses through the night,
With laughter blending in the light.
In the corners, hearts collide,
Each movement, a secret to confide.

They twirl and leap with wild grace,
In this forgotten, sacred space.
Every dancer knows their part,
In this alley, we share our heart.

Skyscraper Shadows

Tall giants stretch into the sky,
Casting shadows as the night draws nigh.
Concrete jungles, dreams confined,
In their depths, hope intertwined.

Windows glimmer like scattered stars,
Holding stories from near and far.
Each reflection tells a tale,
Of journeys that never grow stale.

As the wind whispers through the steel,
We find strength in what we feel.
Among these shadows, we stand tall,
In each heart, a city's call.

Cityscape Chronicles

Skyscrapers touch the sky,
Dreams rise with the sun,
Each window holds a story,
Of battles lost and won.

Traffic hums a tune,
As shadows dance in light,
Concrete jungles breathing,
Through day and into night.

Neon signs are flickering,
Whispers on the street,
Life in every corner,
A rhythm, fast and sweet.

In the heart, a stillness,
Hope lingers like a sigh,
Amid the bustling chaos,
The city's spirit flies.

Tales from the Paved Path

Cobblestones tell secrets,
Of shoes that passed them by,
Each step a silent echo,
Beneath the azure sky.

Sidewalks worn and weary,
Hold dreams beneath their soles,
As voices weave through time,
And laughter fills the holes.

A child skips with delight,
While lovers stroll along,
The path sings stories old,
With every whispered song.

In the tapestry of life,
Each tread a fleeting mark,
The paved path stretches onward,
A journey through the dark.

Whispering Walls

Walls adorned with whispers,
Tales of love and loss,
Paint peels with memories,
Of dreams that bore the cross.

Graffiti tells a story,
Of voices loud and meek,
A clash of hopes and fears,
In colors bold and bleak.

Echoes of the past linger,
In the crumbling bricks,
With every crack and surface,
A narrative that ticks.

In the silence of the night,
They speak without a sound,
The walls hold all the secrets,
Of life that's all around.

Murals of Humanity

Colors splash across the walls,
With stories yet untold,
Murals dance with every hue,
Where hearts and hopes unfold.

Eyes gaze from painted canvases,
Each stroke a silent plea,
To unite the fractured pieces,
Of a shared humanity.

Hands reaching through the layers,
In vibrant shades of grace,
Art becomes a language,
That time cannot erase.

In every corner of the street,
A world begins to bloom,
Murals of our kindness,
Erase the sense of gloom.

The Heartbeat of the Streets

Pavement echoes with feet,
Whispers of dreams and despair.
Beneath neon shadows, we meet,
Stories linger in the air.

Strangers greet with fleeting eyes,
Each corner holds a past unseen.
Streetlights flicker, softly sighs,
Life unfolds, a vivid scene.

Graffiti speaks in colors bright,
Voices rise, a chorus strong.
In the heart of urban night,
We find where we all belong.

Through the chaos, hearts connect,
In the rhythm, we find our way.
Every moment we protect,
The heartbeat of the streets will stay.

Undercurrents of Urban Life

Beneath the surface, currents flow,
Lives entwined in hidden threads.
In the alleys, secrets grow,
Voices travel where hope treads.

Graffiti walls, a silent shout,
Dreams and heartaches intertwined.
In the bustling crowd, no doubt,
Each soul carries stories aligned.

Subway cars hum a soft tune,
Passengers lost in their mind's maze.
Beneath the city's silver moon,
Undercurrents dance in a blaze.

Each heartbeat a whispered prayer,
In shadows cast by city lights.
Together we rise, no despair,
Urban life ignites our nights.

Flickering Candles in a Sprawling Room

In a room where dreams collide,
Flickering candles, shadows sway.
Each flame a wish we cannot hide,
A dance of hope in soft decay.

Walls are dressed in stories worn,
Echoes of laughter, whispers sigh.
From the darkness, we are born,
Together, beneath this sprawling sky.

Candles melt, their wax will fall,
Yet each light holds a memory.
In the twilight, we rise and call,
For every heart's a tapestry.

As the night stretches and bends,
We cherish each flicker, each glow.
In the quiet, our spirit mends,
Flickering candles guide us slow.

Charcoal Dreams

Sketches fade on paper's edge,
Charcoal whispers truth untold.
Lines and curves form a pledge,
In the midst of shadows bold.

With every stroke, a story's spun,
Monochrome landscapes come alive.
In the night, our dreams run,
Ebbing tides where hopes survive.

The artist's heart beats strong and fast,
Each mark reveals a silent scream.
In the present, echoes of the past,
Charcoal dreams ignite the theme.

From darkness, light will bloom anew,
A canvas painted with our fears.
In charcoal night, we find our hue,
Dreams emerge through hidden tears.

Urban Corners

Concrete towers scrape the sky,
Traffic hums as people rush by.
Neon lights flicker, tales unfold,
Stories whispered and sometimes bold.

Sidewalks filled with hurried feet,
Finding solace in the city heat.
Street vendors call with vibrant flair,
Life pulsates in the evening air.

Graffiti blooms on weathered walls,
Echoes of dreams in urban halls.
With every turn, a brand new sight,
City lives intertwined, day and night.

In every corner, moments gleam,
Fragments of life, a shared dream.
Urban tapestry, woven tight,
In these corners, we find our light.

Echoes in the Fog

Misty whispers cloak the streets,
Footsteps echo, silence meets.
Lanterns glow like distant stars,
Hidden stories, life behind bars.

Shadows dance in dusky haze,
Lost in thought, the spirit strays.
Voices murmur, faint and low,
Secrets held in the ebb and flow.

Through the fog, a siren's call,
Distant laughter, a hidden thrall.
Time slips softly, like a dream,
In the mist, we drift and beam.

Echoes linger, tales untold,
In the quiet, we feel bold.
Hope unfurls like morning light,
Guiding us through the endless night.

City Stanzas

In the heart of the bustling throng,
Voices mingle in a vibrant song.
City stories on every street,
Each step taken, a rhythmic beat.

Market stalls with colors bright,
Fragrant spices, a pure delight.
Cafes buzz with laughter's sway,
Moments captured at the end of day.

Bridges span the glimmering flow,
As the sunset paints the world aglow.
City shadows merge and part,
Every corner, a work of art.

Stanzas written in brick and stone,
Urban life, a tale of its own.
With every heartbeat, dreams take flight,
In the city's pulse, we find our light.

Sidewalk Serenades

Guitars strum beneath the trees,
Melodies drift upon the breeze.
Street performers sing their heart,
A serenade, an artful start.

Dancers twirl on pavement's grace,
Rhythms keeping up the pace.
Laughter bubbles, joy unfolds,
In these moments, magic holds.

Fleeting chats and friendly smiles,
Life unfolds in little miles.
Every wave and nod a song,
Together in a world where we belong.

Under the stars, the night ignites,
City dreams in soft moonlights.
Sidewalks hum with love and cheer,
In this serenade, we draw near.

Echoes of Untold Stories

In shadows deep, whispers roam,
Tales of old find their home.
Silent echoes through the night,
Memories painted in moonlight.

Every heartbeat tells a tale,
Of dreams that danced, hopes that pale.
Beneath the stars they softly gleam,
Woven threads of a faded dream.

Voices linger, yet are unheard,
In every rustle, a spoken word.
The past unfolds, a gentle breeze,
History lives among the trees.

Stories cradle each weary soul,
In their depths, we find our whole.
Each breath a glimpse of times gone by,
In the silence, we learn to fly.

Rhythm of Rustling Leaves

Beneath the trees, a whisper flows,
The rhythm of the winds bestows.
Leaves shiver and dance in glee,
Nature's song, wild and free.

Sunlight dapples through the green,
Creating patterns, bright and keen.
A rustle speaks of tales untold,
Of life cycles, brave and bold.

In every flutter, secrets hide,
The gentle winds our timeless guide.
Each sound a step in nature's beat,
The world alive beneath our feet.

Listen close, feel the embrace,
The leaves' soft whispers interlace.
Together they sing, together they sway,
In this serene, enchanting play.

A Canvas of Cobblestones

Every stone tells a tale unique,
Of laughter, journey, and mystique.
Footsteps echo through the years,
Tracing love, laughter, and tears.

The aged paths hold secrets deep,
Memories of those who wander and weep.
In the cracks, life's stories swirl,
In every crevice, time's gentle unfurl.

Moss and shadows softly blend,
Each curve a journey, each turn a friend.
Cobblestones witness the ebb and flow,
Of seasons changing, a life's tableau.

With every step, a breath we take,
In this canvas, dreams awake.
The past alive 'neath our weary feet,
In the cobblestones, our souls meet.

Lanterns of Lost Laughter

In twilight's glow, lanterns sway,
Illuminating night's ballet.
Forgotten joys flicker and dance,
Echoes of laughter in a trance.

Light through glass, a warm embrace,
Reflecting memories, time cannot erase.
Each flame a spark of joy and grace,
Preserving moments, love's soft trace.

Lost laughter whispers through the dark,
A melody igniting a spark.
In every shimmer, stories weave,
Of dreams that linger, hearts believe.

So let the lanterns guide your way,
Through shadows deep, come what may.
In their glow, let memories rise,
A treasure beneath the starry skies.

Cacophony of Solitude

Whispers echo, shadows play,
In the corners where dreams sway.
Alone with thoughts, a silent scream,
Cacophony in this empty dream.

The ticking clock, a distant sound,
Each beat pulls me further down.
An orchestra of lonely sighs,
In solitude, the spirit lies.

Fading light through window panes,
Memories dance in ghostly chains.
I search for comfort in the night,
Yet find no solace, no guiding light.

A murmur swells, a haunting breeze,
Among the ruins, I find my peace.
Cacophony, my heart's refrain,
In solitude, I'm bound by chains.

Bridges of Silence

Spanning waters, the stillness grows,
Where thoughts meander, nobody knows.
Each beam a tether, a bond unseen,
In silence, whispers weave the serene.

Walk with me on this quiet path,
Where echoes linger, but words don't clash.
The air is thick with unvoiced dreams,
Bridges of silence hold the seams.

Beneath the arches, shadows merge,
In this stillness, I feel the urge.
To cross the divide, where hearts reside,
In bridges of silence, side by side.

Moonlit nights guide our way home,
Through starlit skies, we choose to roam.
In every pause, a story lies,
In bridges of silence, love never dies.

Canvases of Asphalt

Underfoot, a tapestry grey,
Stories hidden in the fray.
Brush strokes of tires, a path to trace,
On canvases of asphalt, we find our place.

A dance of feet beneath the sky,
Each step a mark, where memories lie.
In every crack, a tale unfolds,
A city's heartbeat in the cold.

The colors splash in fleeting light,
Cars zoom past, a fleeting sight.
Graffiti whispers, art in the streets,
Canvases of asphalt, where life repeats.

With every season, new stories grow,
Beneath the layers of rain and snow.
In this urban gallery, dreams ignite,
Canvases of asphalt, day and night.

Timeless Pavements

Pavements stretch, an endless road,
Carrying secrets of stories owed.
With every step, the past aligns,
In timeless pavements, history shines.

Footprints linger, faded yet clear,
Echoes of laughter, whispers near.
Each crack and crevice holds a tale,
Timeless pavements, a silent trail.

Underfoot, the rhythm thrums,
Chasing dreams where the pavement hums.
In the warmth of day, the chill of night,
Timeless pavements, our shared delight.

As the seasons shift and change,
Lives intertwine, paths rearrange.
Together we walk, forever aware,
Timeless pavements, a love we share.

Asphalt Serenade

The city hums beneath our feet,
A heart of concrete, bittersweet.
Neon lights and shadows dance,
In this urban maze, we take a chance.

Pavements warm with stories told,
In whispered dreams and silent gold.
Every crack, a tale unfolds,
As sunlight fades, the night beholds.

Beneath the stars, we roam and play,
In this symphony of night and day.
Asphalt rivers, flowing fast,
We chase the echoes of the past.

In this serenade of tires and rails,
A melody where hope prevails.
With every step, a note we share,
In the heart of the city, love is rare.

Metropolis Moons

City lights flicker in the deep,
While tired souls begin to sleep.
The moon hangs low, a silver glance,
As streets below begin to dance.

Skyscrapers stretch, touching the sky,
With dreams of many, reaching high.
In shadowed corners, secrets fester,
Underneath the night's cool luster.

Beneath the stars, we chart our way,
Through alleys where the children play.
The rhythm of life in every beat,
In the pulse of the city, we feel complete.

With every glance, the stories loom,
In the heart of this urban bloom.
The moon our guide, through night we roam,
In this metropolis, we find our home.

Graffiti Hymns

Color splashes on brick walls,
Voices echo through empty halls.
Spray cans whistle a vibrant song,
In the tapestry where we belong.

Artisan hands breathe life anew,
Whispers of hope in shades of blue.
Each mural tells a story bright,
From dawn's first blush to fading night.

In alleyways, a gallery blooms,
Where art breaks chains and clears the gloom.
With every stroke, a truth we find,
In graffiti hymns, we're intertwined.

A symphony of colors sing,
In urban spaces, they take wing.
With every corner, our spirits lift,
In the heart of the city, art is a gift.

Rustic Corners

Beneath the trees, in whispered shade,
Rustic corners where dreams are made.
Old wood creaks in gentle sighs,
As nature bows beneath the skies.

Sunshine dapples on the ground,
In these still moments, peace is found.
With every breeze, a tale is spun,
Of days gone by, of laughter, fun.

Garden paths where wildflowers bloom,
In vibrant colors, filling the room.
Time slows down in these sacred spaces,
Where the heart remembers old embraces.

In rustic corners, life's tender grace,
A place for dreams to softly trace.
With every step, a gentle heart,
Embracing nature, we find our part.

Urban Legends

Whispers in the darkened streets,
Stories gather like lost dreams.
Figures lurking, shadows creep,
Truth buried beneath moonbeams.

A phantom's laugh, a ghostly sigh,
Echoes of those long since gone.
Painted tales in the night sky,
Underneath the city's brawn.

Footsteps that tell of olden fears,
Faces hidden by the flickering light.
Legends drowned in unshed tears,
Veil the monsters cloaked in night.

In alleyways where silence breeds,
Every whisper sparks the flame.
Tales of shadows, haunt our needs,
Creating myths, never the same.

Streets of Solitude

Lonely pathways, empty lanes,
Footsteps echo in the void.
A city lost, barbed with chains,
Silent dreams are now destroyed.

Faded flickers light the way,
In shadows deep, the heart does ache.
Each corner turned, a price to pay,
In this silence, souls will break.

Streetlights flicker, souls collide,
Yet none see the other's face.
In anonymity, we hide,
Chasing phantoms in this space.

The city's hum becomes a song,
But no one hears the melody.
In solitude, we all belong,
Searching for a remedy.

Reflection in Glass

Mirrored surfaces catch the eye,
Fragments of lives pass us by.
Worn-out dreams and whispered wishes,
In every crack, the truth just squishes.

A glimpse of youth, now just a trace,
What was once bright, time's dark embrace.
Hopes rebounding off polished panes,
Life's journey etched in unseen stains.

In reflections, we seek to find,
Echoes of a restless mind.
Shadows dance on the glossy glow,
A silent tale of ebb and flow.

Behind the glass, faces fade,
Stories untold, memories laid.
Illusions clear as we draw near,
What we fear and hold most dear.

Markets of the Mind

Thoughts like currencies, they trade,
Ideas blossoming, never fade.
In crowded stalls of hopes and dreams,
The mind flows with its inner streams.

Whispers barter with silent screams,
A cacophony of broken schemes.
In the bazaar of what could be,
Every choice a mystery.

Memory's stalls, stocked with the past,
Each moment curated, never vast.
Visions tempt like fruits on display,
Yet some desires kept at bay.

A tapestry woven from threads of thought,
In this market, battles are fought.
Yet in the end, what we find true,
Is the heart's longing that knows no due.

The Lens of the Lens

In shadows cast, a vision clear,
A world revealed, it draws us near.
With every click, a story spun,
Life captured bright, two hearts as one.

Through glass we gaze at moments past,
Time held in frames, forever cast.
Each snapshot rich with tales to tell,
In every smile, a secret swell.

Reflections dance in twilight's glow,
Memories linger, soft and slow.
A lens to see beyond the skin,
The depths of souls where love begins.

So let us frame our days in light,
In little boxes, joy takes flight.
With every shutter, life unfurls,
The lens of life, our magic pearls.

Rhythm and Ruin

In abandoned streets, the echoes play,
Rhythms lost in the light of day.
Footsteps haunt where shadows dwell,
A tale of time, a whispered spell.

Cracked pavement sings a tune of space,
Memories linger, time can't erase.
Old walls breathe stories, worn and true,
In silence bold, we hear the view.

Through rusted gates and faded signs,
Nature weaves where once was fine.
A dance of beauty amidst decay,
The heart of art in disarray.

Let's find the pulse of this lost ground,
In rhythm's beat, new life is found.
Amongst the ruins, hope reborn,
In every crack, a seed is sworn.

Paint on Brick

A brushstroke bold, a colorful frame,
Each wall adorned, no two the same.
In every hue, a story starts,
An artist's dream, it speaks to hearts.

Brick by brick, a canvas grows,
In vibrant shades, the city glows.
Whispers of love and tales of strife,
On painted walls, we forge our life.

Through sun and rain, the colors fade,
Yet memories linger, never betrayed.
Each mural speaks of trials faced,
In splashes bright, our dreams embraced.

So let them paint a world anew,
In every corner, a vivid view.
With paint on brick, we leave our mark,
In urban art, we light the dark.

The Sound of City Life

A symphony of footsteps blend,
In bustling streets where strangers mend.
From morning hum to evening sigh,
The city breathes, a living high.

Honking horns and laughter's ring,
As life unfolds, we hear it sing.
Cafes buzz with stories shared,
In every corner, dreams laid bare.

Trains rumble down their metal tracks,
While sirens wail and time relax.
Voices rise, a vibrant choir,
In every note, a heart's desire.

Amidst the chaos, beauty lies,
In every glance, the world complies.
The sound of life, both raw and sweet,
In every heartbeat, the city's beat.

Urban Legends Unfolded

In shadows deep, whispers creep,
Tales of ghosts in the city sweep.
A woman in white, a child's soft wail,
Veils of mystery in the night prevail.

Forgotten alleys, secrets shared,
Each corner holds what few have dared.
Phantom trains on the tracks at night,
Echoing stories lost from sight.

The lighthouse keeper's lonely plea,
Guides lost souls across the sea.
From urban myths, truths emerge,
As whispers fade, legends surge.

In the heart of cities, truths collide,
With every heartbeat, fears reside.
For every tale that paints the dark,
Is a flicker of hope, a hidden spark.

The Heartbeat of Highways

Engines roar on endless tracks,
Wheels spinning, no turning back.
Neon lights in the rear-view shine,
A surge of life, a driving line.

Miles of dreams, roads intertwine,
Voices lost in the radio's twine.
Stars above like guiding eyes,
On asphalt rivers, freedom flies.

Rest stops echo with laughter and sighs,
Hungry hearts beneath wide skies.
The rhythm of journeys, the pulse of time,
Every highway holds a tale sublime.

From city lights to the quiet woods,
The adventure pulses in the hoods.
Each departure marks a new embrace,
In the heartbeat of highways, we find our place.

Bridges of Breath

Over water, steel and stone,
Bridges whisper, connections grown.
Each step taken, a story told,
A journey shared, brave and bold.

Curving arches touch the sky,
Hands held tight as we pass by.
In every breath, a promise made,
Underneath, memories cascade.

The rush of cars, the dance of life,
Unseen forces, joy and strife.
Each bridge a thread in time's embrace,
Binding hearts that seek a place.

Through seasons change, they still remain,
Silent witnesses to joy and pain.
With every crossing, bonds will strengthen,
Bridges of breath, our hearts beckon.

Kaleidoscope of Cultures

In vibrant shades, we blend and weave,
Echoes of stories, none to leave.
Colors clash, yet merge so bright,
Creating beauty in shared light.

From distant lands, a tapestry spun,
Festivals dance when day is done.
Voices rise in harmonious flow,
A celebration of what we know.

Spices mingle on the bustling street,
Each aroma tells who we greet.
Threads of laughter, love, and lore,
In every culture, there's so much more.

With every heartbeat, we intertwine,
A living canvas, yours and mine.
In this kaleidoscope, we shall find,
Unity in diversity, hearts aligned.

Flickering Streetlights

Underneath the city glow,
Streetlights flicker, dance in woe.
Whispers of the night, they sigh,
Echoes of dreams that slowly die.

Pavement cracks in silent plea,
Hold our secrets, can't you see?
Each shadow bends, each move a lie,
Beneath these lights, we wonder why.

In the dark, our stories blend,
With every flicker, paths we wend.
Hopes and fears in twilight strife,
Illuminating threads of life.

Yet through this haze, a spark remains,
A chance for joy amidst the pains.
As long as lights shall ebb and flow,
We'll find our way, we'll learn to grow.

Memories in Motion

Snapshots of times long past,
Moments cherished, fading fast.
Fleeting glances, laughter shared,
In the echo of love declared.

Bicycles raced down dusty lanes,
Sun-soaked days, joyful refrains.
In these frames, we hold so tight,
The spark of youth, a lingering light.

Whispers carried on the breeze,
Frozen smiles, a soft tease.
Through the haze of years gone by,
In every memory, we still fly.

Time may fade, yet we'll remain,
Bound by love, through joy and pain.
In motion, our pasts unfold,
Stories of warmth, forever told.

The Tempo of Uproar

Rhythms clash in urban sprawl,
Voices rise, a chaotic call.
Metronomes of life collide,
In the tumult, we must bide.

Cars rush by, a hurried dance,
Interactions, a fleeting chance.
Laughter spills, the sirens wail,
Within the storm, we set our sail.

A symphony of hopes and fears,
Livelihoods in whispered tears.
Every heartbeat, every shout,
In this uproar, we find our route.

When silence falls, a moment's grace,
In the frenzy, we find our place.
Together in this vibrant roar,
In the chaos, we learn to soar.

Urban Tapestries

Threads of life intertwine and weave,
Stories linger, we all believe.
Street art blooms on crumbling walls,
In every hue, a history calls.

Voices echo in crowded streets,
Cultures mix, a blend that meets.
In each face, a tale untold,
In every heartbeat, courage bold.

Sidewalk markets, aromas swirl,
Colors burst, a vibrant whirl.
Hand in hand, we dance our fate,
In these tapestries, we create.

Sunset glimmers, shadows sway,
In the city's pulse, we stay.
Urban threads, a vast embrace,
Together lost, together grace.

Echoes of History

Through faded halls the whispers roam,
Tales of ages, carved in stone.
Each echo tells of dreams once bright,
Lost to shadows, fading light.

In battles fought and victories won,
In every war, in every sun.
The laughter lingers, the cries remain,
In every joy, in every pain.

Ancient roads where feet have tread,
Now only dust, where once they sped.
Yet time remembers every step,
In every promise, in every prep.

Beyond the veils of time we gaze,
Seeking truth in tangled maze.
The past unlocks its secret door,
As echoes of history whisper more.

Hushed Conversations

In twilight's glow two shadows meet,
Soft-spoken words in rhythmic beat.
The weight of silence speaks so loud,
As heartbeats dance, they form a crowd.

Moments shared beneath the stars,
Places held without the scars.
Each glance exchanged, a secret kept,
In whispered tones, their promise crept.

The world may fade beyond their sight,
In gentle murmurs, taking flight.
With every breath, a bond they weave,
In hushed conversations, hearts believe.

Time stands still, as dreams unfurl,
In quiet spaces, a hidden pearl.
No louder call than silence pure,
In whispered truths, they find their cure.

Mosaics of Memory

Scattered pieces, colors blend,
Fragments of life that twist and bend.
Each shard reflects a moment bright,
Creating beauty from the night.

Patterns form where shadows lay,
Stories told in a vibrant array.
Each tear and laugh shapes the whole,
In mosaics of memory, we find our soul.

Time's gentle hand gives way to art,
As memories dance and never part.
Crafted tales, both wild and free,
In a patchwork tapestry, we see.

Every smile fills the empty space,
Every moment, a soft embrace.
Together they shine, broken yet whole,
Mosaics of memory, the heart's scroll.

Vignettes in Stone

Carved in silence, tales unfold,
In every corner, stories told.
A history captured, firm and strong,
In vignettes of stone, they all belong.

The artist's touch, a fleeting grace,
Transforms the cold to warm embrace.
Each line and curve, each subtle groove,
In these still frames, they seek to prove.

Time weathers all, yet here they stand,
Silent sentinels across the land.
Reminders of life, so rich, so grand,
In vignettes of stone, forever planned.

A moment captured, never to fade,
In timeless echoes, their lives cascade.
Each visage speaks of joys, and moans,
In the heart of history, vignettes in stone.

Nocturnal Narratives

Whispers beneath the starlit sky,
Dreams awaken as shadows sigh.
The moon, a witness to tales untold,
Guides the lost, the brave, the bold.

In alleyways bathed in silver light,
Forgotten secrets take their flight.
Each corner holds a fleeting glance,
As night unfolds its mystic dance.

Voices echo in the deepening hour,
Cloaked in mystery, wrapped in power.
Silent stories from ages past,
Echo in hearts that beat steadfast.

Underneath a canopy of stars,
Every soul holds their hidden scars.
Nocturnal whispers, soft and sweet,
Guide the weary to find their feet.

Mosaic of Memories

Fragments of time, bright and bold,
Kaleidoscope dreams, stories unfold.
Colors blend in a wondrous array,
Each moment cherished, never to stray.

Laughter echoes through sunlit days,
Shadows dancing in playful ways.
The past intertwines, simple but grand,
A tapestry woven by fate's gentle hand.

Photographs fading, yet never erased,
Moments wrapped in love's warm embrace.
Every heartbeat an echo, a sign,
Of lives intertwined, yours and mine.

Time keeps moving, relentless and free,
Yet in each memory, we'll always be.
In the mosaic of life, we find our place,
A symphony of moments, a timeless grace.

Through City Veins

Concrete arteries pulse with life,
A rhythm of joy, a touch of strife.
Neon lights flicker, a vibrant glow,
As the heart of the city begins to flow.

Trains rumble, like thunder through night,
Promises whispered, hopes taking flight.
Skyscrapers whisper in silent tones,
Carrying dreams built on countless stones.

People converge, paths briefly cross,
In every glance, a feeling, a loss.
Stories collide, hearts intertwine,
In the city's embrace, a fate divine.

Through bustling streets, the lifeblood streams,
Each pulse a dance, woven with dreams.
In this urban jungle, we find our ways,
Through city veins, where the spirit stays.

Shadows of Skyscrapers

Tall towers rise, casting deep shadows,
In their embrace, the day softly glows.
Whispers of history cling to the stone,
Tales of those who stood alone.

Dusk wraps around, like a gentle sigh,
As the world below begins to fly.
Lights flicker on, stars take their place,
Mirroring dreams in a busy space.

Footsteps echo, the city's heartbeat,
In the quiet moments, we find our beat.
Each shadow tells of who came before,
In the tapestry woven, forevermore.

Yet in their shadows, we rise and we stand,
Building our futures with hopeful hands.
In the embrace of the past and the new,
Skyscrapers loom, holding dreams that are true.

Breath of Humanity in the Bustle

In the heart of the city, we move as one,
Steps on pavement, under a rising sun.
Faces rushing, stories untold,
Moments fleeting, life unfolds.

Voices blend, a symphony loud,
Dreams interwoven, amidst the crowd.
Children laughing, old souls sigh,
Each breath a whisper, as time flies by.

Neon flickers, shadows dance,
Hearts collide, a fleeting chance.
A shared glance, a fleeting light,
In the bustle, we take flight.

Together we rise, through chaos we roam,
Finding our path, in this concrete home.
The breath of humanity, an unbroken thread,
In every heartbeat, our stories spread.

Chronicles of Crowded Corners

Streets alive with a vibrant hue,
Corners bustling with a world anew.
Street vendors calling, laughter rings,
A tapestry woven from countless strings.

Graffiti whispers tales of the past,
Of dreams that linger, shadowed yet vast.
Footsteps echo on cobblestone paths,
In crowded corners, history laughs.

Sunset paints the sky with fire,
As twilight dances, fueling desire.
In every corner a story waits,
In crowded spaces, destiny congregates.

Amidst the rush, there's beauty to find,
In the heartbeat of the city, all intertwined.
Each busy moment, a thread in the loom,
Chronicles spun, giving life to the room.

Urban Echoes

In the skyline's shadow, we chase our dreams,
A chorus of voices, and distant screams.
Cabs rush by, horns blare their plea,
In urban echoes, we find unity.

Glass and steel rise, reaching for sky,
Reflecting our hopes as some days pass by.
Metro trains thunder, beneath our feet,
Carrying stories, where strangers meet.

Skaters glide, a dance in the street,
While artists paint murals, colors compete.
Each echo a memory, a soft serenade,
In the heartbeat of cities, connections are made.

Under city lights, we gather and roam,
Chasing the night, we find our home.
In urban echoes, we share our days,
A mosaic of voices, in myriad ways.

Concrete Dreams

Between looming towers, dreams take flight,
In the heart of the city, beneath starry night.
Sidewalks busy with stories to tell,
In every heartbeat, we weave our spell.

Graffiti-splashed walls, a canvas alive,
Hopes and desires, where passions thrive.
Laughter and sorrow in the spaces between,
Concrete jungles hold what we've seen.

Each sunrise brings a chance to ignite,
The fire within, to reach for the light.
With open hearts, we dare to aspire,
In concrete dreams, we never tire.

Together we stand, hand in hand,
Building our futures, a united band.
In every moment, we find our theme,
Forging ahead with our concrete dreams.

Illumination in the Alleyways

Flickering lights in the shadows,
Echoing whispers in the night.
Graffiti dreams on brick walls,
Each corner holds a secret bright.

Puddles gleam with moonlit tales,
Mysteries dance in the air.
Soft footsteps on worn cobblestones,
Opening hearts to the rare.

Lanterns sway with a gentle tune,
Casting warmth on faces old.
Beneath the stars, stories bloom,
In the alleys, life unfolds.

Moments shared in fleeting stares,
A connection that feels so right.
Illuminated paths of fate,
Guiding souls through the twilight.

Symphony of Sidewalks

Footsteps echo on the streets,
A rhythm found in every stride.
Voices blend, a bustling beat,
Life's melody can't be denied.

Laughter dances on the breeze,
Children's joy in playful flight.
City sounds a symphony,
Notes of day turn into night.

Street vendors sing their wares,
Sizzling scents fill the air.
Every step, a tune declared,
In this dance, we share and care.

From dawn till dusk, we compose,
An opus woven through the crowd.
A harmony of hearts that rose,
In the city's arms, we're proud.

Twilight in the Town

Hues of orange fill the skies,
As the day begins to sigh.
Shadows stretch, the sun dips low,
In the town, a calm goodbye.

Streetlamps flicker into life,
Casting soft glows on cobbled ways.
Whispers float like gentle waves,
In the stillness, evening stays.

Windows gleam with cozy light,
Families gather, warmth to share.
Hearts unfold with tales of night,
In twilight's hush, a cherished care.

Stars awaken, twinkling bright,
Over rooftops, a canopy.
In this moment, all feels right,
As the town breathes, wild and free.

Metropolis Musings

Steel and glass stretch to the sky,
A jungle of dreams, bold and high.
Rush of life, the pulse of the town,
In the chaos, we won't drown.

Trains rumble like thundering storms,
Carrying stories, hopes reborn.
In the concrete maze, we wander,
Seeking solace, lost in wonder.

Neon lights beckon the night,
A tapestry of colors bright.
Voices mingle, a vibrant hum,
Each moment new, forever come.

In every corner, life unfolds,
The metropolis, a tale retold.
Through the noise, we find our way,
In urban dreams, we choose to stay.

Murmurs Beneath the Surface

Whispers ride the evening breeze,
Heartbeats echo in the trees.
Shadows dance, a quiet thrill,
Secrets linger, gently still.

Ripples form where rivers flow,
Ancient tales the waters know.
Beneath the moon's soft, pale glow,
Life's hidden stories seem to show.

Footsteps trace forgotten paths,
In the silence, laughter laughs.
Every corner holds a song,
Murmurs linger, sweet and strong.

In the hush, a pulse ignites,
Underneath, the world ignites.
Listen close, the echoes call,
Murmurs weaving through it all.

Sidewalks of Stories

Cracks in pavement hold their dreams,
Footfalls dance in sunlight beams.
Every step, a tale unfolds,
Whispers wrapped in bricks of gold.

Children laugh as seasons turn,
Old men sit, their faces worn.
Sketches drawn in chalk and dust,
Lives entwined with hope and trust.

The city breathes beneath the noon,
A vibrant hum, a living tune.
In every stride, a history,
Sidewalks weave their tapestry.

Moments captured, fleeting grace,
In these streets, we leave our trace.
Every story finds its start,
Sidewalks speak from every heart.

Concrete Canvases

Gray and cold, the city stands,
Painted with the artist's hands.
Murals rise, bold visions soar,
Concrete whispers, begging more.

Colors clash and blend with time,
Graffiti speaks in vibrant rhyme.
Stories layered, rich and deep,
In this art, the silence weep.

Walls adorned with tales of strife,
Echoes of a bustling life.
Each stroke captures love and pain,
Reflections of the joy and rain.

Underneath the starry skies,
Concrete dreams will never die.
Every street a work of art,
Canvases that touch the heart.

Secrets of the City

In the twilight, shadows blend,
City's heart will never end.
Veil of night, a cloak of mystery,
Every corner holds history.

Whispers travel through the alleys,
Hopes and fears in silent rallies.
Every window, every door,
Keeps a secret, holds a lore.

Streetlights flicker, softly gleam,
Echoes of a lost dream.
Hidden lives beneath the stars,
Life's enigma written in scars.

Wander on, let stories flow,
In between the highs and lows.
Secrets linger, softly bind,
In the city, truth you'll find.

Urban Echoes

In the city's heartbeat, echoes play,
Neon lights flicker, night turns to day.
Voices collide, laughter and sighs,
Hidden in shadows where time often flies.

Pavements are rivers of stories untold,
Dreamers and thinkers, both young and old.
Every corner whispers the past and the now,
In the urban jungle, we wonder just how.

Sirens wail melodies, the traffic hums,
Every late-night diner, a place where life comes.
Skies painted orange, dusk settles in,
Amongst the chaos, the peace will begin.

We'll dance to the rhythm, chase fortune and fate,
In the heart of the city, we'll never be late.
For every echo that fades into air,
Is a promise of memories we're destined to share.

Skyline Serenades

Beneath the vast canvas, where dreams take flight,
The skyline stands tall, a beautiful sight.
Windows like eyes, reflecting the dawn,
Songs of the city, from dusk until dawn.

Clouds brush the rooftops, whispers of blue,
Stories unfold, between me and you.
Balconies sway with the rhythm of life,
In the heart of the city, joy cuts like a knife.

Skyscrapers echo each laugh and each tear,
In the embrace of the night, we conquer our fear.
Stars flicker gently, a wink from above,
Binding our souls with a thread of pure love.

And when the dawn chases shadows away,
We'll bask in the promise of a bright new day.
The skyline sings softly, our dreams it conveys,
In this serenade of urban displays.

Concrete Whispers

Between the bricks, stories pulse and breathe,
Concrete whispers secrets, if we just believe.
Graffiti echoes hearts that once beat loud,
Nature's persistence, among the proud.

Sidewalks crack open with tales from the past,
Lives intertwined, their shadows are cast.
Pigeons coo softly, beneath iron beams,
In this bustling harbor of hopes and dreams.

Footsteps weave patterns, a dance on the stone,
Each path taken is never alone.
Streetlights flicker and guide, like stars they glow,
Through urban jungles where winds gently blow.

Whispers of laughter, of grief and of grace,
In this concrete maze, we each find our place.
A symphony rises from the heart of the street,
In every whisper, life's rhythm we meet.

Streets of Stories

Every street corner holds a tale so dear,
From laughter to loss, we gather near.
Cafés and markets, alive with delight,
In the streets of stories, we find our light.

Bricks tell of lovers, the young and the bold,
A treasure of memories, waiting to unfold.
Vividly painted, the murals speak loud,
Of struggles and triumphs that make us proud.

Children's laughter dances on the breeze,
Echoing dreams, sweet as honeyed teas.
With every small step, we write our own page,
In the book of the city, we share a stage.

As dusk sets in, the lanterns ignite,
Casting warm glows, a comforting sight.
In these streets of stories, our hearts will unfold,
With every new chapter, we become more bold.

Hues of Humanity

In every face, a story told,
The warmth of kindness, the strength in bold.
A tapestry woven with threads of fate,
Each shade unique, together we create.

From laughter bright to sorrow's tear,
We dance through trials, year by year.
United in spirit, we rise and stand,
With open hearts, we reach for hands.

The colors blend in harmony,
A mural of dreams, a symphony.
In every heartbeat, love appears,
Binding us close, quelling our fears.

So let us paint with brushstroke grand,
The hues of life, both bold and bland.
For in our differences, we find a start,
A masterpiece created by every heart.

Echoes of Laughter

In the gentle breeze, laughter flows,
A melody sweet, where joy bestows.
Children's giggles in the fading light,
Chasing shadows, igniting the night.

From gardens bright to bustling streets,
Happiness blooms, where friendship meets.
Whispers of joy through rustling leaves,
A symphony sung by hearts that believe.

Every chuckle, a spark of cheer,
Moments cherished, year after year.
In the warmth of smiles, we find our way,
Together we'll dance, come what may.

So let the echoes ring far and wide,
In every soul, let laughter reside.
For in each giggle, we catch a glimpse,
Of life's true beauty, in joyful rhythms.

Pathways of Dreams

Beneath the stars, where wishes play,
We wander roads, come what may.
Each step a rhythm, each turn a chance,
In the dance of fate, we take our stance.

With hopes like lanterns, we light the night,
Guided by visions, our hearts alight.
The journey unfolds, a map of desire,
Chasing horizons that never tire.

Through valleys low and mountains high,
We seek the truth in the vast sky.
Each dream a whisper, each thought a guide,
On pathways we're destined, side by side.

So let us wander, let us explore,
For in the quest, we find so much more.
With open hearts and spirits bold,
We'll write our stories, in dreams untold.

Underground Journeys

In caverns deep, where shadows dwell,
A world awakens, with secrets to tell.
The earth's heart pulses, in rhythmic beats,
Through ancient tunnels, where wanderers meet.

Drifting through darkness, feeling the stone,
Each echo a memory, never alone.
With lanterns bright, we crave the light,
Guided by whispers that soften the night.

The roots of time stretch far and wide,
In this hidden realm, where the past abides.
Through chambers vast, we seek and find,
The stories of ages, in whispers confined.

So delve into depths, let curiosity roam,
For in underground's embrace, we find home.
With every step, a new tale to see,
A journey unfolding, forever free.

Serendipity in Side Streets

Winding paths beneath the trees,
Whispers float in evening breeze.
Hidden gems in shadows play,
Life's small treasures found each day.

Corner cafes, laughter shared,
Unexpected moments dared.
Serendipitous, sweet surprise,
In quiet nooks, the heart complies.

Footsteps dance on cobblestone,
Stories linger, seeds are sown.
In the humble, joy abounds,
In the noise, the magic found.

With each turn, the world expands,
Life unfolds in gentle hands.
Serendipity leads the way,
In side streets where dreams hold sway.

Harmony of Hectic Lives

In the rush, we find our song,
Beating hearts where we belong.
Cities pulse with life and light,
Together in the endless fight.

Side by side on crowded trains,
Shared connections, silent gains.
Harmony in every face,
Unity amidst the race.

Frantic mornings, fleeting time,
Rhythms rise, a vibrant rhyme.
In chaos, we discover peace,
A bond that will never cease.

Through the noise, our dreams take flight,
We find solace, bright as light.
In this dance, we're intertwined,
A harmony of hearts aligned.

Urban Soliloquies

In the city, thoughts unfold,
Silent whispers, tales retold.
Each street corner holds a muse,
In solitude, our minds can cruise.

Neon lights, a starry glare,
Lost in musings, unaware.
The hum of cars, a lullaby,
In urban silence, dreams can fly.

Sidewalks echo with our sighs,
In the bustling, truth complies.
Thoughts meander, time stands still,
Where the heart and mind canthrill.

With every step, reflections grow,
In the shadows, secrets flow.
Urban soliloquies we share,
In the city's breath, we dare.

Lantern-lit Pathways

Glow of lanterns, soft and warm,
Guiding souls through night's calm charm.
Footsteps light on gravel stones,
In the darkness, no one's alone.

Whispers of the evening air,
Stories linger everywhere.
Paths illuminated, dreams take flight,
In the solace of the night.

Flickering flames against the chill,
Hearts entwined with time to fill.
In each shadow, love's embrace,
Lantern-lit, we find our place.

As the stars begin to gleam,
In these paths, we chase our dream.
Together in this tranquil light,
We walk the pathways of the night.

Twilight Conversations

In the hush of the evening glow,
Words linger soft, whispers flow.
Stars blink in the velvety sky,
Hearts share secrets, time slips by.

Shadows stretch, as dreams unite,
Moments captured, holding tight.
Glimmers of hope in twilight's embrace,
Each glance a promise, a warm trace.

Voices dance in the cool night's air,
Gentle laughter, free from care.
Beneath the moon, the world feels right,
In twilight's charm, we find our light.

As stars fade into morning's hue,
These twilight talks, forever true.
With every heartbeat, connections swell,
In the silence, love's stories tell.

Vibrations of the Void

In the depths where silence sings,
Echoes pulse with hidden things.
Whispers of the cosmos call,
In the void, we sense it all.

Darkness carries a gentle sound,
In stillness, mysteries abound.
Ripples dance in heavenly space,
Lines of fate we cannot trace.

The universe breathes, a soft sigh,
Stars illuminate the open sky.
Each vibration holds stories vast,
Connecting present, future, past.

In this realm, we find our peace,
From chaos, a wondrous release.
Through the void, we learn to see,
The magic in life's mystery.

Corridors of Connection

In narrow paths where shadows meet,
Lives entwined, moments sweet.
Every glance, a shared embrace,
In corridors, we find our place.

Fingers brush, a serendipitous touch,
Hearts resonate, longing so much.
Walls echo soft laughter's sound,
In these spaces, love is found.

Each step forward, a timeless dance,
In the corridors, we chance romance.
With every heartbeat, stories flow,
In these halls, emotions grow.

As we wander, paths unfold,
Tales of connection, forever told.
In every doorway, hope resides,
Through connected lives, joy abides.

Echoes of Everyday

In morning light, the world awakes,
Simple joys the day makes.
A child's laughter, a bird's sweet song,
In everyday life, we belong.

Coffee brews, a comforting scent,
Moments caught, time well spent.
Elderly hands, stories to share,
Within each glance, love and care.

The busyness buzzes, yet still we find,
Beauty in chaos, a peace of mind.
In mundane tasks, magic hides,
In echoes of life, happiness abides.

As day turns to dusk, the cycle flows,
In everyday rhythms, our spirit grows.
Through laughter and tears, we weave our way,
In the echoes of life, we choose to stay.